Creative Snacks, Meals, Beverages and Desserts You Can Make Behind Bars:

A Cookbook for Inmates
(and others on a tight budget)
looking to put the fun back into food

Kevin Bullington

Creative Snacks, Meals, Beverages and Desserts You Can Make Behind Bars:

A Cookbook for Inmates
(and others on a tight budget)
looking to put the fun back into food.

Copyright 2013 by
Kevin Bullington

For Mom

This cookbook was made to introduce you to a new style of eating. The prison population in America is steadily rising. Because of that and the nationwide budget cuts, meals in prisons are getting cheaper. Think processed "mystery" meats and soy imitations. Think endless bins of overcooked squash.

The canteen stores are usually the only way an inmate can eat something that doesn't turn the stomach but 40 cents a day is not going to get you much. Most inmates depend on their families to send a little something every week or month. With a little creativity, inmates have developed a way to cook and eat food that reminds them of what they're missing in society.

I was incarcerated for nine years and came across many really good recipes. I thought I'd share them with people in prison, and also with people in the "free world" who are trying to feed themselves on a budget.

Prison life varies from place to place and, like anywhere else in life, there is good and bad stuff going on. Cooking is definitely something good. It's a great way to pass the time, feel better and bring people together.

Some foods in this book are not the healthiest in the world. This book will not help you lose weight or lower your cholesterol. It's just a way to try something new and tasty and different. I hope you find something in here you really like.

And, for the rest of the world, remember, that inmates are usually living in unusual circumstances, forced to make the best out of a bad situation, and searching for moments of hope and accomplishment big and small as they work to turn their lives around. The more support they have from the outside world, the more likely they'll be to succeed.

Table of Contents:

- Swolls   8
- Lasagna   12
- Pizza   15
- Chicken with rice   17
- Pork fried rice   19
- Fish Casserole   21
- Wraps   23
- Nachos   28
- Chili cheese fries   30
- Chicken Cheese Wraps   32
- Pizza burger   34
- Things you can add to
  Soups, cheeseburgers
  and sandwiches
  to dress them up   36-38
- Ooh Whop/State cake   39
- Honeybun sandwich   45
- Honeybun melt   47
- Ice cream and cookies   49
- Ice cream pie   51
- Cappuccino   53
- Iced coffee   55
- Lollipops/suckers   57
- Taffy   59

SWOLL

A Swoll is a commonly eaten meal in the prison system. It's quick and easy to make, no matter if you're feeding yourself or eating with several others. The combination of ingredients are so easily altered that it is hard to grow tired of this cheap and delicious meal that could easily become popular in regular society. Perfect, for example, for college students or anyone else without much spare time and living on a tight budget.

It is basically the combination of ramen noodles, cheese, chips or crackers, vegetables and meat. Sometimes rice is added. There are numerous variations to be tried.

Ingredients for making 1-person portion, regular flavor Swoll

4 chicken-flavored ramen noodle soups
1 beef summer sausage
1 can chili with beans
1 medium bag of Cheetos
½ an onion
2 cups of boiling hot water
2 small, clear plastic trash bags

Directions:

Cook ramen noodles separately in their Styrofoam containers. Crush noodles, add seasoning and boiling water. Crush bag of Cheetos into powder. Cut summer sausage into pieces as big or small as you like. Cut onion as you prefer. Put chili into bowl and heat in microwave until hot. Put onion slices into a bowl with a little butter and heat in microwave. Add onions and sausage to chili and warm in microwave. Put two small clear plastic trash bags inside of each other. Pour extra water out of soups and dump all noodles into plastic trash bags. Add all remaining ingredients and use hands to mix all contents in bag. When everything is mixed, wait five minutes.

Ingredients for making 5-person Ultimate Swoll

20 chili ramen soups
4 large beef summer sausages
4 cans of chili with beans
1 whole onion
1 whole green pepper
2 pickles
2 blocks of cheddar cheese
Water for boiling noodles
2 small, clear, plastic trash bags

Directions:

Cook ramen noodles separately in Styrofoam cups. Crush noodles, add seasoning and boiling water. Cut cheese into slices and then cut slices in half twice. Cut onion, green pepper and pickles into pieces that are as big or small as you like. Add pieces of onion, green peppers and pickles into a bowl with some butter. Heat in microwave. Cut sausages into pieces and add into bowl with chili. Heat chili and sausage. Put two small clear plastic trash bags inside of each other. Pour extra water out of finished soups and dump noodles into trashbags. Add all remaining ingredients to bag and use hands to mix all contents in bag. Spread bag on table and knead with hands. When contents are mixed, wait five minutes. Scoop noodles into bowls for everyone to eat and enjoy.

Prison Ingredients Used in Swolls:

Bacon
Fried chicken
Chili with beans
Hamburger steak
Tuna
Turkey
Red hot turkey sausage
Summer sausage
Sausage patty
Jalapeno peppers
Green peppers
Onions
Pickles
Shredded cheddar cheese
Squeeze cheese
Pepper jack cheese
Grilled cheese crackers
Cheetos
Ramen noodles (various flavors)
Rice

LASAGNA

Lasagna is one of the most creative and delicious meal ideas I have seen in prison. It's fun to make and really tastes great. It's a little more expensive than most meals and takes some ingredients that are not easily obtained, which is why it is not as popular as other meals. Ketchup is only available in packets passed out with the purchase of microwavable foods. 30 ketchup packets are needed to make the sauce.

Ingredients to make lasagna:

1 cup of boiling water
1 cup of hot water
3 bowls (1 large and at least six inches deep)
3 soft shell tortilla wraps
3 grilled cheese crackers
3 chili ramen noodle soups with seasoning
2 country link sausages
2 squeeze cheeses
30 packs of ketchup

Directions:

Crush up noodles. Cut up meat. Add pack of
seasoning to noodles. Add noodles, seasoning and
meat to bowl (use the smaller bowl for this step)
and mix well. Get new bowl and squeeze 30 packets
of ketchup into it. Add a pack of seasoning to
ketchup. Add half cup of hater water and mix with
spoon. Crush up grilled cheese crackers and add to
bowl. Mix in with spoon until sauce thickens. Add
½ cup water to noodles. Cook noodles in
microwave for 2 minutes (halfway through, mix
noodles with spoon). Get large, circular bowl at
least six inches deep. Boil a cup of water. Using
glove or tongs, dunk one tortilla shell in from top
and bottom for five seconds. Place soft, wet shell at
bottom of large bowl. Spread a spoonful of sauce on
top of tortilla. Spread out about half of noodles and
meat on tortilla. Spread evenly and pack with
spoon. Add about half of sauce on top of noodles
and spread evenly. Use one entire squeeze cheese
package on top of sauce. Squirt evenly around top
and spread with spoon. Dunk second tortilla in
water a little longer than first time. Place wet shell

on top of cheese layer evenly. Repeat noodles. Repeat sauce. Repeat squeeze cheese. Dunk third and final tortilla in water for about 10 seconds. Add shell to top. Spread one spoonful of sauce on top. Cut into four pieces with knife all the way through. Put in microwave for six minutes. Remove and let cool. Use big spoon to remove.

PIZZA

Fun to make and good to eat. Definitely a must for those pizza fanatics who gotta have a slice every now and then to get that monkey off their backs. (This is another recipe that requires 30 ketchup packets.)

Ingredients to make one small pizza

Pack of soft shell tortilla wraps
3 squeeze cheeses
30 packets of ketchup
3 grilled cheese crackers
1 beef summer sausage
1 pack of pepperoni
1 block of cheddar cheese
Shredded cheddar cheese

Extra ingredients for pizza:

Sliced onion
Sliced green pepper

Directions:

Put 1 tortilla wrap on a plate. Spread one pack of squeeze cheese onto shell. Add a second shell on top of first. Cheese should hold wraps together. Add another pack of squeeze cheese to top of second wrap. Add a third shell. Crush crackers and mix with ketchup and squeeze cheese. Spread sauce on top of third wrap. Crumble block of cheese onto sauce. Sprinkle shredded cheese onto sauce. Cut sausage into little pieces. Heat sausage pieces and pepperoni in microwave. Add to top of pizza and warm to melt cheese. Add extra ingredients if you have them. Use knife to cut into slices.

CHICKEN AND RICE

A big meal, perfect for when you want
something that tastes great and will fill you up.

Ingredients to make chicken and rice (feeds 2)

6-piece microwaveable fried chicken box
2 jalapeno squeeze cheeses
Spicy vegetable ramen noodle seasoning pack
Hot pickle
4 grilled cheese crackers
bag of white rice

Directions:

Dice up pickle and save the juice. Cook whole bag of rice as directed. Pick apart chicken pieces. Throw away skin and bones. Put meat in bowl. Mix chicken meat in with rice. Add squeeze cheese and mix. Warm mix in microwave. Sprinkle seasoning into mix. Add pickle to mix. Crush crackers and sprinkle on top.

PORK FRIED RICE

If you miss Chinese food, there is still one dish you can have. A smart imitation that tastes as good as the real thing.

Ingredients to make pork fried rice

Half a bag of white rice
3 spoons of butter
2 country link sausages
½ an onion
pack of spicy vegetable ramen noodle seasoning

Directions:

Dice ½ an onion. Cook onion slices with butter in microwave. Cook rice as directed. Cut sausages into pieces. Add Butter and seasoning to rice and fry in microwave. Make sure to stir. Add sausage and onions. Warm in microwave.

FISH CASSEROLE

A good, filling meal that will leave you satisfied. The type of fish depends on what you have available. Tuna, mackerel and fish steaks are the most common. If you can get anything out of the kitchen, you might want to try that.

Ingredients to make fish casserole

shrimp ramen noodle soup
white rice (amount is up to you)
pack of tuna or mackerel or fish steaks
jalapeno squeeze cheese
pack of grilled cheese crackers
2 packs of mayonnaise
¼ of an onion
bag of Jalapeno potato chips (can substitute
other flavor chips as needed)

Directions:

Dice up onion. Cook soup and rice separately as
directed (pour out extra broth and water). Mix
soup and rice into one bowl. Mix in fish. Crush
up crackers and mix in. Cook onion slices in
microwave with butter. Add onion to mix. Add
mayonnaise and mix. Spread cheese on top.
Crush chips and sprinkle on top.

WRAPS

A very simple and tasty meal or side dish depending on what it is that you're doing. The most popular recipe is basically cooking a Swoll and adding it to a soft shell tortilla wrap with some squeeze cheese. I am going to be offering you the special version, which is less used because the ingredients are harder to come by. There are many variations and I encourage you to find a unique style that fits your tastes. I just want to share the best ones I've come across and pass that knowledge along to you.

Ingredients for making1-person, chicken-flavored wrap meal (makes 3 wraps)

1 pack of chicken breast chunks.
1 pack of soft shell tortilla wraps
1 block of pepper jack cheese
½ an onion
½ green pepper

Directions:

Dice up onion and green pepper into small pieces. Add pieces to bowl with small spoon of butter. Heat in microwave and mix so butter covers pieces. Heat long enough to soften onions with hot butter. Get another bowl and add chicken chunks. Cut up cheese into small slices and mix in with chicken. Heat in microwave to melt cheese into chicken. Add onion and pepper to bowl with chicken and mix. Heat until hot. Soften tortillas by heating in microwave. Add chicken mix to wraps proportionately. Fold wraps.

Ingredients for making 1-person beef summer sausage wrap

1 medium beef summer sausage
1 bag of refried beans
rice and cheese
1 block of cheddar cheese
½ an onion
1 pack of soft shell tortilla wraps

Directions:

Add refried beans to bowl and add right amount of boiling water. Dice up onion into small pieces. Add onion to bowl with spoonful of butter. Heat and mix until onions are covered with butter. Heat until butter softens onion. Cut summer sausage into pieces. Cut cheese into slices. Mix cheese and sausage in bowl. Heat in microwave to melt cheese into sausage. Add rice, onion, and meat all into one bowl to mix. Heat until hot in microwave. Soften tortillas by heating in microwave. Add sausage mix to tortilla shells. Fold wraps.

Ingredients for making 1-person fish wrap meal

2 packs of tuna
½ an onion
2 hot squeeze cheeses
½ bag of plain rice
Ramen noodle shrimp soup
Pack of soft tortilla shells
Spoonful of butter

Directions:

Crush ramen noodles. Add seasoning pack and water to soup. Save enough seasoning to sprinkle on rice. Add water to rice and let cook. Dice onion into pieces. Add butter to onion pieces in a bowl. Heat onion in microwave and mix hot butter around. Heat until onion is softened by hot butter. Sprinkle soup seasoning onto rice and mix in. Add ramen noodle soup to bowl with rice and mix. Add tuna and mix. Add onions and mix. Heat in microwave to warm up. Soften tortilla shells by heating in microwave. Add one pack of squeeze cheese to wrap filling mix. Spread other cheese onto tortilla shells. Add fillings and fold wraps.

Ingredients for making 1-person breakfast wrap meal

2 servings of scrambled eggs
½ an onion
½ a green pepper
½ bag of rice
9 slices of bacon
9 slices of cheese
pack of beef flavored soup seasoning
spoonful of butter
pack of soft shell tortillas

Directions:

Dice onion and green pepper into pieces. Mix with spoonful of butter and heat in microwave until soft. Add water to cook rice. Mix rice and eggs in bowl. Sprinkle in beef seasoning. Add onion and green pepper to eggs and rice. Heat in microwave till hot. Put 3 slices of cheese on each wrap. Put 3 slices of bacon on each wrap. Warm wraps in microwave. Add fillings to wrap and fold.

NACHOS

This is something usually only made on special occasions like during sports games. It is easy to make and tastes great. It didn't take too much imagination to come up with but the prison version can really be as good as anything made in the free world.

Ingredients to make nachos

chili with beans
refried beans with rice
squeeze cheese
pickle
onion
green pepper
tortilla/nacho chips
medium clear plastic bag

Directions:

Spread bag out on table. Cut pickle, onion and
green pepper into pieces. Cook chili with beans in
microwave. Add water to refried beans with rice
and heat in microwave. Squeeze the cheese into
bowl or cup with pepper and onions mixed in. Heat
in microwave. Spread chips out across bag on table.
Spread chili on top of chips. Spread beans and rice
across chips. Spread cheese across chips. Spread
pickle across chips.

CHILI CHEESE FRIES

Another snack perfect for eating while watching a sports game. A little messy but you won't mind, even if you spill a little on your shirt.

Ingredients to make chili cheese fries

¼ onion
pack of chili with beans
2 boxes of microwaveable crunchy french fries
1 pack of squeeze cheese
cup of shredded cheddar cheese
Bag of dehydrated fried beans
Spoonful of butter

Directions:

Dice onion. Cook onion slices with butter in microwave. Cook refried beans as directed. Add onions and chili to a separate bowl. Cook fries as directed. Mix chili with onions and refried beans. Put both boxes of fries onto one plate. Pour chili mix on fries. Squeeze cheese on top. Sprinkle cheddar cheese on next. Warm in microwave.

CHICKEN CHEESE WRAPS

Probably the tastiest of anything on this list. It
certainly stands out among the top favorites. I
would expect everyone to fall in love with this
meal.

Ingredients to make chicken cheese wraps (3 wraps)

Pack/can of pure breast chicken chunks
block of white pepper jack cheese
pack of Cajun chickens ramen noodle seasoning
1/2 an onion
1/2 a green pepper
bag of white rice
slice of butter

Directions:

Cut onion into slices. Cut green pepper into slices.
Put onion and green pepper slices into bowl with
butter. Heat in microwave to soften slices. Cook
rice as directed. Put chicken chunks into bowl.
Crumble block of cheese and add with chicken.
Heat in microwave to melt cheese. Sprinkle Cajun
flavor onto rice. Warm tortilla shell in microwave.
Add onions and peppers to chicken and cheese. Add
rice to tortilla shell. Put chicken mix on top of rice.
Fold wraps.

PIZZA BURGER

After you eat so many regular microwaveable cheeseburgers or small, single serve pizzas, they start to lose their taste. Combine the two and you have something new and delicious.

Ingredients to make pizza burger

microwavable single serve frozen pizza
microwavable double cheeseburger

Directions:

Cook pizza in microwave as directed. Cook
cheeseburger in microwave as directed. Put pizza
between meat of cheeseburger.

Best eaten with:
bag of chips, candy bar and soft drink

THINGS YOU ADD TO A RAMEN NOODLE SOUP TO DRESS IT UP:

Bacon
Baked chicken
Chicken patty
Fish steaks
Hamburger steak patty
Mackerel
Sausage link
Summer sausage
Tuna
Turkey red hot
Vienna sausage
Beans and weenies
Cheddar cheese
Pepper jack cheese
Squeeze cheese
Cheetos
Chili powder
Green pepper
Jalapeno peppers
Onion
Pickles
Regular cheese nacho chips
Various kinds of crackers
Rice

THINGS TO ADD TO A MICROWAVEABLE CHEESEBURGER:

Bacon
Fried Egg
Doritos
Green pepper
Jalapeno pepper
Ketchup
Lettuce
Mayonnaise
Onion
Tomato
Pepper Jack cheese
Squeeze cheese
Salt and vinegar chips
Sour cream and onion chips

THINGS TO ADD TO COLD SUBS AND SANDWICHES:

Bacon
Turkey
Ham
Eggs
Doritos
Green peppers
Lettuce
Mayonnaise
Mustard
Onions
Tomatoes
Pepper jack cheese
Squeeze cheese
Salt and vinegar chips
Sour cream and onion chips

"STATE CAKE" OR "OOH WHOP"

While there are many different combinations for main course meals with meat, bread and cheese, there are really only a select few dessert choices. The State Cake stands out as the ultimate prize for satisfying a sweet tooth. The combinations and flavors are many and depend upon what is available in the canteen. You are basically taking jumbo honeybuns and wrapping them together in a dough you've made out of cookies and candy bars.

You can be creative and add different fillings, like cream or jelly. And you can play with the flavors of the dough. I have made and tasted many variations and, when done right, an "Ooh Whop" can really be something special.

Where inmates are forced to use the limited ingredients and tools available to them, I encourage cooks in the free world to be creative and take the "Ooh Whop" to the next level once you have created and tasted the traditional prison recipes.

The possibilities are endless. I can only imagine how good a State Cake could be with marshmallow cream and peanut butter filling!

Ingredients for regular flavor, 1-person "State Cake" or "Ooh Whop" cake:

2 regular or iced jumbo honeybuns
1 pack of chocolate chip cookies
1 Snickers bar
1 cup of water
1 small plastic trash bag

Directions:

Crush up cookies in small plastic trash bag. Tear up Snickers bar into pieces and add with crumbled cookies. Add just enough drops of water to dampen crushed cookies. Mash into a dough. Roll dough out as flat as you can. Take honeybuns and place together on top of spread out dough. If iced, make sure to put the iced sides touching each other. Using bag, fold and wrap dough around honeybuns. Use spoon to spread dough around edges.

Ingredients for peanut butter flavor with Reese's Peanut Butter Cup filling, 1-person cake

4 packs of peanut butter cookies
1 pack of Nutter Butter cookies or 1 cup of peanut butter
2 jumbo iced honeybuns
2 chocolate Reese's Peanut Butter Cups
1 cup of water
1 small, clear plastic trash bag

Directions:

Crush up peanut butter cookies in clear plastic trash bag. Add just enough water to dampen crushed cookies. Mash into a dough. Roll dough out as flat as you can (can be made to your choice of thickness). Take one honeybun and place in center of dough, iced side up. If you choose to make a peanut butter paste from Nutter Butter cookies, you must crush up cookies and add a few drops of water, just like you did when you made the dough. When finished, spread paste on iced sides of both buns. If you use real peanut butter, you may want to heat what you're using in the microwave for several seconds to loosen it up a little so that you don't tear up the side of the bun when spreading peanut butter. Place Reese's Cups between iced sides of buns. Fold and wrap dough around buns. Use spoon to shape dough around edges.

Ingredients for lemon cream filling, 1-person cake:

4 packs of vanilla cookies
4 packs of lemon cookies
2 jumbo iced honeybuns
1 cup of water
small Styrofoam cup
small plastic trash bag

Directions:

Crush up vanilla cookies in bag. Add just enough water to dampen crushed cookies. Mash into a dough. Roll out dough as thick or thin as you prefer. Take one honeybun and place iced side up in center of dough. Take apart every lemon cookie and scrape off lemon cream filling with a plastic knife. Collect cream fillings in small Styrofoam coffee cup. When finished, spread cream on iced sides of both buns. Put buns iced sides together in center of dough. Spread, fold and wrap dough around buns. Use spoon to shape dough.

Ingredients for strawberry flavored, 1-person cake

2 jumbo iced honeybuns
4 packs of strawberry cookies
2 Strawberry Shortcake Rolls (Little Debbie)
1 cup of water
1 small, clear plastic trash bag

Directions:

Crush up strawberry cookies in bag. Add just enough drops of water to dampen crushed cookies. Mash into a dough. Roll dough out as flat as you can get it. Place honeybun iced side up on dough. Place strawberry rolls side by side on iced side of honeybun. Take second honeybun, iced side down and press down on rolls. When honeybuns are together, fold and wrap dough around buns. Use spoon to spread dough around buns.

PRISON INGREDIENTS USED IN DOUGH:

chocolate chip cookies
cookies and cream bars
Hershey's chocolate bars
lemon cream cookies
MilkyWay bar
peanut butter cream cookies
Snickers bar
strawberry cream cookies
vanilla cream cookies
Zero bar

PRISON INGREDIENTS USED IN FILLINGS:

lemon cream
oatmeal pie cream
peanut butter
Reese's Peanut Butter Cups
strawberry cream
strawberry rolls
vanilla cream

HONEYBUN SANDWICH

Perfect when you need something sweet that can really fill you up.

Ingredients to make honeybun sandwich

white iced jumbo honeybun
peanut butter
jelly
2 slices of white bread

Directions:

Spread peanut butter and jelly on both slices of bread. Put honeybun in between bread.

Goes good with:

Chocolate milk
jungle juice

HONEY BUN MELT

One of the easiest and quickest sweets there is to make. If you don't have a lot of time or just can't wait to eat something sweet, then this is the thing for you.

Ingredients for making honeybun melt:

plain or iced jumbo honeybun
Pack of Reese's Peanut Butter Cups

Directions:

Place honeybun on plate. Place peanut butter cups on top of honeybun. Microwave for 30 seconds.

OTHER THINGS THAT CAN BE PUT ON HONEYBUN MELT:

chocolate granola bars
Snickers bars
other candy bars

ICE CREAM AND COOKIES

Another simple but delicious idea for anyone with a
sweet tooth. It's best eaten on a hot summer day.
Will help keep you cool and happy.

Ingredients for ice cream and cookies special

1 pint of cookies and cream ice cream
1 pack of chocolate cookies with vanilla cream
filling
1 pack of M&M's
1 Snickers bar

Directions:

Scoop ice cream into a bowl with a little extra
room. Crush cookies and sprinkle onto ice cream.
Tear Snickers bar into pieces and place around
bowl. Add M&M's to top of ice cream.

OTHER INGREDIENTS TO MIX AND MATCH:

Any flavor ice cream
Peanut M&M's
Reese's Pieces
any candy bar
any flavor cookies

ICE CREAM PIE

An absolutely amazing treat, best served in the summer. You try this one and you'll never forget it!

Ingredients to make ice cream pie

1 pint of vanilla ice cream
1 banana
cinnamon
1 apple Danish
butter
sugar

Directions:

Cut banana into slices. Sprinkle cinnamon onto
slices. Spread a spoonful of butter on slices.
Sprinkle sugar onto slices. Heat in microwave. Heat
Danish in microwave. Cut open Danish and put in
bowl. Scoop ice cream onto Danish. Poor banana
slices onto ice cream while warm. Sprinkle
cinnamon and sugar on top.

CAPPUCCINO

When you need a jolt of energy that tastes great or when you need a sweet drink to keep you warm on cold nights.

Ingredients for cappuccino (1 cup)

Spoonful of instant coffee or 4 instant coffee packs
4 coffee creamers
2 packs of instant hot cocoa with marshmallows
6 packs of sugar

Directions:

Boil cup of water. Add instant coffee and stir. Add creamer and stir. Add sugar and stir. Add cocoa and stir.

ICED COFFEE

This is an awesome way to start your day.
Especially on those warm summer days. It is very
easy to make if you have access to ice and sugar.
Will definitely give you a jolt of energy and, once
you taste it, you won't be able to wait to have
another one.

Ingredients for iced coffee

4 hot chocolate packs with marshmallows
2 spoonful(s) of instant coffee
20 packs of sugar
1 cup full of ice

Directions:

Add hot chocolate, coffee and sugar to cup of hot
water. Stir well and let cool. When cool, pour into a
cup filled with ice.

HOMEMADE SUCKERS

A creative treat you will really enjoy. Make some for you and your friends and your friends will beg you to make them again.

Ingredients to make homemade suckers

1 bag of Jolly Ranchers
1 bag of Now & Later or Starburst candy
a cap for the mold of the sucker
wax paper

Directions:

Get a bag of Q-tips and cut the cotton ends off. Put stick into Starburst or Now & Later. Put Jolly Ranchers into bowl and melt in microwave. Find a cap to be the mold. Add wax paper to the cap. Have stick with candy side down in middle of cap. Pour Jolly Rancher mix into cap and let cool.

TAFFY

Another perfect idea to share with others. A must
for candy lovers.

Ingredients to make taffy

1 bag of Country Time Lemonade
lots of coffee creamer
sugar

Directions:

Add a cup of coffee creamer to a bowl. Add ¼ cup
of lemonade. Add ¼ cup of sugar. Add just a few
drops of water. Stir until mixed. Spread onto a plate
to harden. Shape how you want it. Let sit overnight.